THE TALE OF AQHAT

The Murder of Aqhat (Part II, ii.)   *British Museum*

The Tale of
AQHAT

Translated with an Introduction by
FRANCIS LANDY

THE MENARD PRESS
1981

THE TALE OF AQHAT

Introduction, translation, notes © 1981 Francis Landy

Preface © 1981 David Daiches

Acknowledgement is due to the Imprimerie Nationale, and Paul
Geuthner, who published *Le Corpus des tablettes en cuneiformes
alphabétiques découvertes à Ras Shamra*, Vol.X, ed. Herdner, Paris, 1963,
from which the cover picture and frontispiece are taken.

Acknowledgement is due to the Arts Council of Great Britain
for their 1980-1981 grant to The Menard Press

The Menard Press is a member of ALP

ISBN 0 903400 62 6

North America distributor: Small Press Distribution Inc.,
1636 Ocean View Avenue., Kensington, Cal. 94707 USA

THE MENARD PRESS
8 The Oaks
Woodside Avenue
London N12 8AR

*Printed by Skelton's Press Ltd.,
Wellingborough, Northamptonshire, England.*

Preface

IN some ways the Bible, or at least that part of it known as the Old Testament, has been a great blocker of light. Its grandeur and authority, its canonical position in both the Jewish and the Christian world, its acceptance as something absolutely unique and incomparable, have for long stood between post-biblical man and an awareness of his pre-biblical cultural roots. One of the great achievements of modern Semitic studies has been to enable us to cross to what Francis Landy calls 'the other side of the ideological barrier of the Bible.' Archaeologists, linguists, ancient historians and anthropologists have between them in the last half century illuminated the culture of peoples in the ancient Middle East whose achievements were for long obliterated by the Israelites and the Bible they produced. In Israelite eyes the Canaanites whom they supplanted were cultural enemies, dealers in abomination, as different from themselves as they could possibly have been. But we now know, thanks to the discoveries and investigations of modern times, that Israel's cultural enemies and predecessors lived in many respects in the same world of myth and attitude. The Ugaritans in particular, who were Canaanites, though they speak to us from behind the biblical barrier, can now be seen to have inhabited a world that has all kinds of links with other ancient Middle Eastern cultures not excepting that of the Israelites themselves.

Of course the Tale of Aqhat, with its frank polytheism and positive luxuriating in what might be called human weaknesses of gods, is in these respects very remote from anything biblical and closer to aspects of the ancient Hellenic world. Indeed, the relationship between Semitic and Hellenic myth patterns is one of the most interesting things that emerges from a study of the Tale of Aqhat, even in the fragmentary form in which we have it. Not only is it fragmented, it is also in parts if not unintelligible at least not certainly intelligible, as Mr. Landy explains in his introduction and notes. Nevertheless, what we have of it is still an exciting and illuminating epic poem, whose flavour comes across remarkably well in Mr. Landy's translation. The reading of such a work enlarges our perspective of the ancient world and enables us to set familiar cultural phenomena in a setting that is wider both chronologically and geographically than the one we are accustomed to see them in. The work is also humanly interesting for its own sake. Reading it helps us to expand the canon of classic literature as it has been developed over the Christian centuries and see new aspects of the ancient world in all their fascinating differences from and similarities to those we were brought up on.

Mr. Landy's translation of a difficult and often uncertain text is done with linguistic tact and genuine poetic feeling, as well as with a sense of the whole background against which the text can be read. It is an exciting contribution to our new knowledge of the ancient world.

DAVID DAICHES

Introduction

I UGARIT AND ITS PEOPLE

Near Latakia in Syria is a promontory known as Ras Shamra or 'Fennel Head'. Here in 1929 an Arab peasant struck a Mycenean tomb while ploughing; excavation revealed a late Bronze Age city, identified as the well-known Ugarit. In the High Priest's house a large library was discovered, containing epic poems in a hitherto unknown script. Its decipherment is a marvellous story, (see, for instance, Cyrus Gordon's *Forgotten Scripts*, Thames and Hudson, 1968). From the documents that have been recovered – diplomatic, commercial, intimate, sacred – we have learnt much about the civilisation of Canaan i.e. the Mediterranean littoral from Turkey to Egypt, against which the Israelites strove; in other words, we see the Bible from a pagan perspective. The history of Ugarit is very short – from the invention of the script in c.1400 to its destruction in about 1200 B.C. – but very significant. It brings us to the threshold of the Bible, since the first Hebrew texts that survive date from perhaps 1250 B.C., and it coincides also with the most exciting and informative period of Egyptian history, that of the el-Amarna tablets, the revolution of Akhenaton, the tomb of Tutankhamun. It is also very rich.

An absorbing summary of the politics, trade, religion and splendour of Ancient Ugarit is to be found in the *Cambridge Ancient History* (rev.ed.) Vol.II. ch.21 iv & v (fascicle 63): 'Ugarit' by Margaret S. Drower (Cambridge U.P. 1968). I advise readers who are truly interested to turn there. It was a great commercial, cosmopolitan centre, linking the Aegean with the Near East, with organised communities of Egyptians, Cypriotes, Cretans, Hurrians, Hittites and others, and a second language – Hurrian. Its royal palace covered 2½ acres; only that of Tyre could compare with it. It worshipped a loose and unstable pantheon (c.250 deities have so far been discovered). Baal, the great enemy of the

7

Hebrew YHWH, the god of fertility, rain and social order, and Dagan, the corn god, were the most revered, with the largest temples. In the myths, Baal secures an uncertain victory over Chaos, represented by the Sea, and struggles indecisively against Death. Above is El, the supreme god as in the Bible, ambivalent in his sympathies, worshipped in no temple, strangely ineffectual. There is no trace of child-sacrifice, and little of temple-prostitution, both of which characterised later Phoenician religion; but much drunkenness.

For most of the period Ugarit was a dependency of the Hittite Empire, and it fell with that Empire also, in the great convulsion of the still mysterious 'Sea-Peoples' that brought the Bronze Age to a close. Part of the Sea-Peoples became the Philistines. Ugarit loyally sent her entire army to help the Hittite Emperor in his extremity; part of her fleet was wrecked in a storm; others were far away. Thus she was quite defenceless. Still in the oven were found a hundred clay tablets, unbaked, telling of the panic of those last days.

2   ITS LANGUAGE AND SCRIPT

Ugaritic is a branch of North-West Semitic, closely related to Hebrew, Aramaic, Phoenician, and the newly discovered Eblaitic. Its script is an alphabet – itself an innovation in the second millenium – and is inscribed on clay tablets, using the cuneiform technique of the Babylonians. An example can be seen on the photograph. The script read from left to right, like English but unlike Hebrew and other Semitic languages; the little ticks, looking like tiny pear drops, that can just be discerned in the photograph are word-dividers. The scribes were not very consistent about this, and often omitted the word-dividers in compound phrases. Added to the difficulty of reading the script, worn down by 4000 years, is that of the language; despite the usefulness of comparative etymology, and the tremendous achievement of the philologists, the meaning of many words remains in doubt, since they often occur only once or twice, and in broken contexts. Like Hebrew and Egyptian, Ugaritic is mostly unvocalised; this creates enormous problems of ambiguity. If English were written in Ugaritic, for example, *s* could signify *as, is, us* and *so,* as well as the genitive and the plural. In Ugaritic, *l,* as well as being a vague preposition meaning both *to* and *from,* and vocative *O* (e.g. O king), is a particle of both negation and affirmation. Hence some passages are open to diametrically opposed interpretations. For example, some commentators hold that Anat's 'He shall not live!' on p.28 is in fact 'He shall live!' or 'He shall revive!'

Another source of ambiguity is the lack of any form of punctuation, so that syntactic divisions are often uncertain. This is compounded by the frequency of lacunae; owing to the fragmentary state of the tablets, reconstruction is often necessary and possible, though full of pitfalls. Most of what I have translated has been partially reconstructed on the basis of parallel passages and contextual likelihood. For example, of the divine banquet at the beginning of Part I Section iv only a few words and phrases are extant; nevertheless, these are identical to those in a similar passage in the Baal-Anat Cycle, from which the whole description has been 'lifted'. For Ugaritic epic literature, like that of Homer, is highly conventional, and had a repertoire of stock formulae, which it would use whenever appropriate.

3   THE TALE OF AQHAT

The Tale of Aqhat was found, together with the other two epics, the Baal-Anat Cycle and the legend of Keret, in the library of the High-Priest's House, excavated in the first seasons. It had been recorded shortly before an earthquake destroyed half of Ugarit in 1365 B.C.; the calligraphy suggests that the scribe is the same as the one who transcribed the other two texts, namely Ili-milku the Shubanite.

9

It is very incomplete; three tablets were found, and one cannot even speculate as to its original length. Of these three tablets only the third is reasonably complete; the middle two columns of the first have been broken off, and only a corner of the second survives. The surface of the tablets is very abraided and covered in pockmarks; hence it is very difficult to read, and the beginning and end of the columns are worn away, or broken off.

The epic begins with the ritual Daniel undergoes to obtain a son; its success and his joy. The motif of the righteous man who is childless and granted a son by God is familiar from the Bible; one thinks of Abraham, Isaac and Samuel. The son miraculously conceived is 'marked' by divinity; and this is compounded by the visit of the Kathirat, the conception deities in the form of swallows, and the gift of the marvellous bow by the craftsman-god, Kothar-wa-Hasis. The magical endowment of fertility initiates the dialectic of the poem, between life and death, seasons of growth and decay, which it shares with the two other great Ugaritic poems. The subsequent bereavement makes the miracle ironic, cancels it out; the very bow that confirmed divine favour is the instrument of divine destruction. The same pattern is to be found, in a yet more terrible form, in the Sacrifice of Isaac, where the father is commanded to kill his own promised and God-given son.

The first part of the Tale is at pains to emphasise Daniel's perfection: he is assiduous in his devotions to the gods, he protects the widow and orphan, and knows how to entertain divine visitors. Aqhat, indeed, is explicitly a reward for his virtue. Thus the question of theodicy is interwoven with that of death and fertility. It centres, however, round the figure of Aqhat himself.

The first sections have an incantatory quality, with their repeated portraits of the ideal son and his somewhat sordid duties, the ritual of incubation, the entertainment of Kothar-wa-Hasis. It is only very slowly that the narrative takes shape. This may, however, be a distortion owing to the absence of the middle two sections, which were presumably an account of Aqhat's birth and childhood, and the origins of the divine bow. At the very end of the third section, when Daniel gives Aqhat the bow, there is a very poignant reference to his first kill through hunting; for the first victim of the bow will be Aqhat himself.

The next section begins with a divine banquet at which the goddess Anat sees Aqhat's bow and determines to obtain it. From the incredible drunkenness of the assembled pantheon – at another celebration El wallows in his own shit – Anat emerges, irresponsible, deadly, obsessed. Later her henchman, Yatpan, will be betrayed by drink; the sinister becomes comic. Anat offers silver and gold for the bow, and Aqhat refuses; then she offers him immortality. It is not clear whether it is hers to give, or a callous trick, as Aqhat claims. His sharp retorts show either courage or rash ignorance of his peril; for Anat glories in scenes of tireless slaughter, in which she wades up to the neck in the blood of her enemies. As Aqhat declares that man is essentially mortal, punning on the words for 'death' and 'man', we are aware that Anat hates being crossed, and cannot experience death. Aqhat identifies himself with all men and speaks for them, as he asserts his rights against her inhuman and unlimited power. It is stressed that he is ideally beautiful and noble, man's most perfect specimen; but his fatalistic dignity is mingled with all-too-human fallibility and youthful intemperance. The superciliousness of his jibe 'A warrior's bow: do women hunt with it?' reminds us of another young rational hero confronted with the daemonic, Pentheus in the Bacchae. Like Pentheus, Aqhat dies for his irreverence, is dismembered and eaten, as was the victim in the original Bacchanalia.

Aqhat cannot foresee the consequence of his refusal, especially since El, Yatpan, and finally Anat herself, in bitter contrition, protest against its injustice. We do not know what he would choose, nor whether the bow is worth his life. For him it is a sign of the divine grace that marked him at birth. In a very interesting article, the only one, to my knowledge, to delve into the inner meaning of Ugaritic texts, Delbert R. Hillers* suggests that the bow is a symbol of Aqhat's virility, and that the whole episode is a conflict between the all-powerful castrating female – terribly attractive and dangerous – and the young and innocent male, a theme familiar both in ancient mythology and in neurotic literature throughout the ages. I think that his argument is valid and convincing, but capable of extension. The bow is a metonym for Aqhat, inseparable from him, and when he dies it is lost or breaks. Moreover it becomes clear that the real object of Anat's affections is Aqhat himself; she admires him, proposes marriage, and grieves for him. The bow is a projection of Aqhat, outside himself; it conceals and protects him, interposed between himself and Anat, and communicates between them; ironically, he is its first victim. It is the occasion for all the very considerable and subtle ambiguity of this passage; Anat flatters and offers herself sexually to Aqhat as a trick to obtain a bow, but in fact she transparently deceives herself, the trap is a wish-fulfilment. Like Freudian jokes, deceptions reveal unconscious motives and dilemmas. But the bow is more than Aqhat's emblem; it is also the creation of Kothar-wa-Hasis, the craftsman god, and ideally beautiful. For this reason Anat covets it. Finally, the bow stands for a sexual difference, as Aqhat tactlessly remarks, and for the male preserve of hunting; however, with it sexual energy becomes aggressive and destructive.

The ironic point of this impertinence: 'A warrior's bow: do women hunt with it?' is precisely this, that Anat is the

* D. R. Hillers, 'The Bow of Aqhat: The Meaning of a Mythological Theme'. *Orient and Occident: Essays presented to Cyrus H. Gordon on the occasion of his Sixty-Fifth Birthday*, ed. Harry A. Hoffner Jr. AOAT 22 (Verlag Butzon and Bercker Kevelaer, Neukirchen-Vluyn 1973) p.71-80. It incurred a characteristically febrile and feeble denunciation from a diehard philologist H.P. Dressler (Ugarit Forschungen [1975] 217-20).

goddess of hunting as well as a ferocious warrior. She wears male clothing, and dyes herself red like a warrior; there is speculation that she was androgynous*. Like Ishtar and the Roman *Venus barbata,* she is sometimes pictured with a beard. Aqhat's mocking question is surreptitiously crucial: he insists on the absolute difference between men and gods, man and woman. Anat, on the other hand, is bisexual, and offers to abolish those differences, to make Aqhat immortal. The sexual exchange of marriage would literally disarm him, enable Anat to possess his virility (the bow = phallus), his identity (the bow = Aqhat), and the divine part of him. For Aqhat's essential attribute is not his at all, and distinguishes him from other men; in a sense Anat is reclaiming it/him for divinity.

Anat cannot stand being thwarted, she refuses to accept the regulation of the limits between individuals that comprises justice, she believes that she has a right to everything that she desires. She may stand, as Hillers suggests, for the all-powerful female, insatiable and inescapable, in whom the psychoanalyst would recognise the echo of the archetypal mother, omnipotent, possessive, androgynous, from whom the child strives precariously to maintain a separate existence. On the other hand, she is absolutely infantile, an infant who has never learnt to curb her wishes. This strange reversal, typical of the paranoid position, is the disastrous formula round which the epic turns.

Anat, infuriated, goes to El to demand vengeance; when he apparently refuses, she threatens him and all his children with general destruction, and he rather tamely complies. This happens rather frequently in their relationship – the tempestuous daughter and the weak, somewhat senile

*J. C. de Moor, in *Seasonal Patterns in the Myth of Ba'lu according to the Version of Ili-milku* (Neukirchen, 1971) p. 132-193. and 'Problematical Passages in the Legend of Aqhatu' Ugarit Forschungen 7 (175) p. 171-215. AOAT 16 (Butzon and Bercker Kevelaer, Neukirchen-Vluyn 1971).

father. El's surrender contrasts with Aqhat's defiance, especially since he is nominally the guardian of justice, the supreme authority. Behind both responses is the problem of man's relationship to the daemonic, which he can neither deny nor fully express; indeed, how to cope with evil.

We know very little about the following episodes, because they have almost entirely vanished; only that they introduce the theme of the cycles of the moon, and concern hunting. If they were extant, we would have a clearer idea of the sexual relationship of Anat and Aqhat. The text resumes to describe his murder, by Anat through her agent Yatpan in the guise of eagles. Later, the remains of Aqhat are found in the belly of Semel, the mother of eagles. There is an apparent equivalence between Semel and Anat; Anat, the archetypal mother who wished metaphorically to devour Aqhat. Sexual tension turns to murder, its double and opposite; Anat incorporates Aqhat, destroying him, and losing the bow also.

There follows a long sequence in which Aqhat is mourned, first by Anat, then by Daniel and Pughat, Aqhat's sister. As a result of the murder, the crops fail, and Daniel and Pughat visit the fields, invoking rain. Crime and fertility are interconnected, as in the Bible; the pitiful death of the young here corresponds sympathetically to that of the young shoots. In each field there is a solitary green stem; Daniel pathetically wishes that Aqhat will harvest it. Pughat is prescient, and leads him weeping; the sad procession is interrupted by messengers bearing the news of Aqhat's death. Daniel finds his remains, and curses the cities near which he was killed. Then, after seven years' grief, Pughat sets forth to avenge his murder.

Pughat's epithets 'Who fetches water, gathers dew to swell the barley, knows the courses of the stars' indicate familiarity with the seasons and fates, an affinity with the forces of redress and vitality, that through her the disjunction between earth and heaven will be healed. Aqhat provokes Anat unawares; Daniel ironically hopes that

14

Aqhat will remove the blight and complete the harvest; Pughat, on the other hand, 'knows the courses of the stars', and realises immediately what has happened. At the appropriate time, and after incense has been offered to those stars, she takes action. Her epithets associate her with Anat, who 'washes in the dew of heaven . . . the stars.' Moreover, on her venture she disguises herself as Anat, and assumes a male role, that of the avenger of blood*. It is an interesting structural feature, implying a hidden symbolic connection, that Anat pretends to be Aqhat's sister, while Aqhat's sister pretends to be Anat, in both cases to accomplish a murder. Yatpan meanwhile claims to be like El, and his boast and drunken fearlessness suddenly reminds us of El's quavering compliance to Anat's threats. He abuses the laws of hospitality, in contrast to Daniel's meticulous welcome of Kothar-wa-Hasis and the other gods at the beginning of the epic. Everything is moving to a climax when the text breaks off.

4 THE REPHAIM TEXTS

Most commentators assume that Aqhat was ultimately resuscitated, and there is confirmation of this from the fragmentary Rephaim texts, obscure and largely duplicating each other, which may be part of the sequel to our story. In them the Shades are summoned by Daniel to a feast; El revives them, and someone – de Moor postulates that it is Aqhat – is crowned king. It is difficult to comment on texts whose content and context is so uncertain; nevertheless, they do suggest a resolution not only of the personal tragedy of Aqhat, but of the wider question of man's existence after death, as a semi-divine wraith, mediating between men and gods.

---

* The last section of the poem is one of the most ambiguous and disputed, and anything said of it has to be qualified. Therefore I have kept my remarks short.

5 RELATED LITERATURE AND MYTHOLOGY

This is an extensive and well-explored subject, on which only a few comments are possible here. Investigation has developed on two paths: the search for similar stories and similar names. For instance, Cyrus Gordon finds the names of both Aqhat (Kehath – Moses' grandfather) and Pughat (the good Israelite midwife Puah) in Exodus. Delbert Hillers, as noted, presents a paradigm of stories, from Gilgamesh and Ishtar to Joseph and Potiphar's wife. A very interesting source of parallels is *Hellenosemitica**, by Michael Astour. Astour's thesis is that pre-classical Greece was under considerable Semitic influence, both in culture and population, and in part he endeavours to establish this through an exceptionally detailed comparative study of myth. He considers that Aqhat is Actaeon, Semel is Semele, Daniel Danaos. Actaeon and Semele are related: Ctaeon was Semele's nephew. Astour proceeds to find remarkable parallels between the myths associated with these figures, and the Tale of Aqhat. Ultimately, one may envisage a comparative analysis similar to that of Levi-Strauss for the mythology of South America; but this perhaps is wishful thinking.

6 THE TRANSLATION

Translation is hard, often bitter, sometimes joyous, long disagreeable days followed by others when one strikes the right note. Of course it is 'free', in the sense that a literal translation of poetry is completely unfaithful to its spirit; on the other hand, I have rarely strayed far from the original meaning and structure. Epic poetry is formal, with set phrases and vocabulary; where their equivalents have lost all their resonance in English, others must be found. A

---

* An Ethnic and Cultural Study in West Semitic Impact on Mycaenean Greece (Brill: Leiden 1968).

problem is that of metre: Ugaritic poetry, like Hebrew, is constructed round parallelism, with a variable equivalence of stress-groups in each colon. After much hesitation, I adopted metre as the formal equivalent of parallelism in European literature, endeavouring to keep it flexible and to adapt it to the changing rhythm of the original. For instance, I turn tetrameters into trimeters where the Ugaritic lines shorten.

In any case, it will be clear by now that the meaning of the texts is highly speculative, an exact translation, in the fullest sense, impossible. Nevertheless, I have been very fortunate to have obtained the advice of an Ugaritic expert, Mrs. Sandy Littman, but for whose penetrating and often acerbic comments the translation would have looked rather different. Of course she bears no responsibility for the errors that still remain; especially on points where we disagree. Nevertheless, I have relied exclusively on previous scholarly translations, in English, French and Hebrew. In particular, I have used *Textes Ougaritiques** and 'Problematic Passages in the Legend of Aqhatu' and by J. C. de Moor and M. Dijkstra *Ugarit Forschungen* 7 (1975) pp 171-215. The latter is especially valuable for its daring interpretations of passages no one else has attempted.

---

* *Textes Ougaritiques:* Tome 1: '*Mythes et Légendes.* Introduction, Traduction, Commentaire by André Caquot, Maurice Szuycer, Andrée Herduts (du Cerf, Paris, 1968).

The Tale of Aqhat

I

(i)   Daniel of Harnam, man of healing
Lord of the Shades, the valiant hero,
Entertained the gods with feasting,
Quenched the thirst of the holy ones.
He took off robes, he went and lay down,
Loosened his loincloth, slept the night.
A day passed, two days passed.
Daniel entertained the gods,
Entertained the gods with feasting,
10   Quenched the thirst of the holy ones.
Three days, four days passed.
Daniel entertained the gods,
Entertained the gods with feasting,
Quenched the thirst of the holy ones.
Five days, six days passed.
Daniel entertained the gods,
Entertained the gods with feasting,
Quenched the thirst of the holy ones.
Daniel, then, uncloaked,
20   Uncloaked he went and lay down,
Loosened his loincloth, slept the night.
Now, after seven days,
Baal, stirred to pity, came close by:
'Forlorn is Daniel, man of healing,
The valiant lord of Harnam grieves:
He has no son, child of his loins,
No root like his brothers, his kinsmen.
Let him not be without a son,
A root like his brothers, his kinsmen.
30   He entertains the gods with feasting,
Slakes the thirst of the holy ones.
Bless him, my father, El the Bull,

Comfort him, Creator of Creatures.
Grant that the house cradle a prince,
An heir in the heart of the palace.
To raise a solemn stone for ancestors,
For the departed, a sun-disk;
To draw his wraith like vapour from the earth,
And guard his shrine from impious hands;
40 To silence those who cast aspersions,
And drive them out who scheme against him;
In drink to take his hand,
When wine-flushed to bear him;
To eat his spelt, his offering,
In Baal's house, in the house of El;
To thatch his roof in rainy weather,
To cleanse his clothes on stormy days.'
The chalice held between his hands,
El blessed Daniel, man of healing,
50 Grace for the valiant lord of Harnam:
'As my soul lives, may Daniel live!
Health to the man of healing!
Strength to the lord of Harnam!
May his way prosper!'
Daniel went to his bed, lay there,
Kissing his wife, caressing her;
Feverish she conceived,
Roused to the glow of conception,
To the heat of generation,
60 For the man of healing,
Lord of the Shades.
Thus was the house quick with a son,
A seed in the heart of the palace,
To raise a solemn stone for ancestors,
For the departed, a sun-disk;
To draw his wraith like vapour from the earth,
And guard his shrine from impious hands;
To silence those who cast aspersions,
And drive them out who scheme against him . . .

(There is a gap of about twenty lines of text (c.30 lines of verse).
When the text resumes, a messenger is bringing the good news to Daniel).

(ii)   '. . . To the departed, a sun-disk;
        To draw your wraith like vapour from the earth,
        And guard your shrine from impious hands;
        To silence those who cast aspersions,
        And drive them out who scheme against you;
        To eat your spelt, your offering,
        In Baal's house, in the house of El.
        In drink to take your hand,
        When wine-flushed to bear you;
10   To thatch your roof in rainy weather,
        To cleanse your clothes on stormy days.'
        Daniel, his face radiant,
        Gleaming his forehead, dimpled,
        Broke into smiles, and laughed,
        Feet thumping the footstool,
        His voice exulting, cried:
        'I will rest, I will be at peace,
        Quiet in my breast will be my soul,
        For a child will be born to me,
20   A root like my brothers, my kinsmen,
        To raise a solemn stone for ancestors,
        For the departed, a sun-disk;
        To draw my wraith like vapour from the earth,
        And guard my shrine from impious hands;
        To silence those who cast aspersions,
        And drive them out who scheme against me;
        In drink to take my hand,
        When wine-flushed to bear me;
        To eat my spelt, my offering,
30   In Baal's house, in the house of El;
        To thatch my roof in rainy weather,
        To cleanse my clothes on stormy days.'
          Daniel rose, came to his house,
        His palace Daniel entered.

His rooms filled with the Kathirat,
The swallows, daughters of gladness.
Then Daniel, man of healing,
Lord of the Shades, of Harnam,
Slaughtered an ox for the weavers of music,
40 Fed the Kathirat, weavers of music,
Slaked the thirst of the daughters of gladness,
The swallows.
One day, two days,
He fed the Kathirat, weavers of music,
Slaked the thirst of the daughters of gladness,
The swallows.
Three days, four days,
He fed the Kathirat, weavers of music,
Slaked the thirst of the daughters of gladness,
50 The swallows.
Five days, six days,
He fed the Kathirat, weavers of music,
Slaked the thirst of the daughters of gladness,
The swallows.
Then, after seven days,
The Kathirat left the house,
The swallows, daughters of gladness,
Those who alight on beds of joy,
Conception and childbirth they follow.
60 Daniel sits and counts her months,
Months come and go . . .
. . . come and go . . .
. . . three, four . . .

(Two whole columns are missing. In the meanwhile, Daniel's son Aqhat is born. Kothar-wa-Hasis, the craftsman god, is speaking:)

(iii) '. . . There I will bring a well-strung bow,
Four arrows in a quiver.'
Seven days passed.
Then Daniel, man of healing,

Lord of the Shades, of Harnam,
Rose, sat at the flared gate,
The threshing-floor, superb with princes.
He judged the widow justly,
The orphan's grievance fairly,
10   Then, lifting up his eyes,
He stared:
                in the immense distance,
                over clear space,
                Kothar coming!
He gazed, gazed further:
                The path of Hasis coming!
A bow he bore him.
See! Shaft and quiver!
20   At this, Daniel, man of healing,
Valiant Lord of Harnam,
His wife called, jubilant:
'Lady Danatay, listen!
A lamb prepare, pound corn,
Refresh Kothar-wa-Hasis,
Feast Hayin, the intricate Craftsman!
Regale the gods! Pour drink,
Revere them, honour them,
Lord of the realm of Ptah,
30   Of all of it, God . . .'
        Lady Danatay listens,
Dresses a lamb, pounds corn,
To feast Kothar-wa-Hasis,
Refresh Hayin, the intricate Craftsman.
Kothar-wa-Hasis come by and by,
Daniel receives and holds the bow,
The shaft and quiver on his knees.
Lady Danatay thereupon
Regales the gods, pours drink,
40   Reveres them, honours them,
Lord of the realm of Ptah,
Of all of it, God . . .

Kothar set forth for his pavilion,
Hayin took leave, and went back home.
Then Daniel, man of healing,
The valiant lord of Harnam,
Took the bow, named it and blessed it,
For Aqhat he named it, and bound it:
'Your first kill,
50   Your first kill,
O my son, my son,
Into the palace . . .'

(There is a lacuna of about forty lines).

(iv)   The gods are feasting, drinking;
They dine off milk-fed lambs,
Succulent flesh, cut with salt knives.
Draughts of wine they drink in flagons,
The blood of grapes in cups of gold.
They fill their cups, fashioned in silver,
Drain flagon after flagon.
The stewards, ever busy,
Bring bubbling new wine into Baal's house,
10   Into El's house: the old is finished.
Jar pours on jar.
    Drawing the shaft back, taut and steady,
Aqhat aligns the marvellous bow,
Devised by Kothar-wa-Hasis,
Skilled in speaking, cunning in carving.
    She lifted up her eyes, and gazed;
Anat stared at the bow of Aqhat.
Fair was its form, lovely to look at,
Its glittering arrows raced the lightning,
20   Lightning that teases cowering waters.
Anat wished to align the bow,
To aim the arrows, taut and steady,
The skilled work of Kothar-wa-Hasis.
Horns carved like serpents twist and stare.
The beaker falls from Anat's hand,

24

The flagon from her fingers spills,
In the dust wine trickles.
She lifted up her voice and cried:
'Listen, noble Aqhat, listen!
30 Silver is yours, if you should wish it,
Gold, if you prefer! Only give me . . .
Give me your bow, grant me your quiver!'
    And noble Aqhat answered:
'The finest ash of Lebanon,
The finest tendons of wild oxen,
The finest horns of swift gazelles,
Filaments from the thighs of bulls,
And the fine reeds from the wide marshes,
Give these to Kothar-wa-Hasis,
40 And let him frame a bow for you,
A quiver for the Widow,
Sister-in-law of Nations.'
    The fair Anat replied:
'Wish, Aqhat, wish; life will I send you —
Ask, hero, ask; deathless I make you.
There you will number years with Baal,
Count seasons with the sons of God.
As Baal, when he returns to life,
When all is ready,
50 Expectant,
The Master-player gives him to drink,
He plays and sings, shapes spells about him,
A sweet voice plays, I tell you truly –
I offer noble Aqhat life for ever!'
    Then noble Aqhat speaks:
'Do not deceive me, O fair maiden,
Your lies are hateful to a hero.
Death is man's fate,
What will he take?
60 What will he take?
Death is man's way,
A white glaze on my head,

25

Ash sprinkled on my crown,
The death of all, my death,
With the dead I will die.
I will say yet more: I will ask you –
A warrior's bow: do women hunt with it?'
     Anat's mouth is full of laughter,
While her heart is wry, and schemes:
70 'Consider well, my noble Aqhat,
Consider well, retract your answer!
On paths of pride lest I should meet you,
In stubborn ways lest I should find you,
Under my feet lest I should trample you,
Loveliest, most virile of men!
     Her feet whirr as she leaves the earth,
She travels to the Source of Rivers,
Surge of abysmal waters,
Passes into the royal compound,
80 Retreat of God, Father of Years.
She fell prostrate before his feet,
Worshipped, and paid him homage.
Bitterly she reviled Aqhat,
Daniel's darling, man of healing.
She lifted up her voice, and cried:
          '. . . Aqhat . . .
             . . . him . . .'

(15 lines missing)

II

i)   *(the first five lines broken)*

Then said Anat, the flawless Virgin:
'Let not your sons, O El,
Let not your sons rejoice,
Your children in your palace.
For my right hand will seize them,

My fist will pound them, crush them.
Your skull shall shatter from my blow,
Your grey hair will be dyed with blood,
Your venerable beard with gore.
10 And Aqhat, shall he save you?
From Anat's grasp deliver you,
Daniel's child, on the day you call?'
El spoke, compassionate ever:
'I know you, my contemptuous daughter,
Virile and fractious, as no goddess;
Evil flares in your heart, my daughter.
Go your way, do your will,
Your passionate purpose accomplish!
Suppress him who defies you,
20 As threshed wheat, tread him down!'
Anat laughed, the flawless Virgin.
Then she set forth for noble Aqhat,
Across clear space, an immense distance.
Anat laughed, the flawless Virgin.
She lifted up her voice and cried:
'Listen, noble Aqhat, listen!
You be my brother,
Make me your sister;
Bring seven retainers,
30   . . . my father . . .
King, you'll go a-hunting . . .
I will teach you hunting . . .
              . . . Qeret-Abilim . . .
     Weeping City of the Moon

(The rest of the column, the next two, and half of the fourth are missing).

ii)   . . . shrilling . . .
     Off went Anat, the flawless Virgin.
She made her way to Captain Yatpan,
She lifted up her voice, and cried:
'Yatpan, be seated;
              . . . Qeret-Abilim,

27

Weeping City of the Moon . . .
Who will renew the moon?
                    . . . its right tip . . .
10   Shatter . . . his skull.'
Yatpan demurred, liege to the lady:
'Listen, Anat, the flawless Virgin.
Should you kill Aqhat for his bow?
For his quiver should he perish?
He lays the feast, so fair to look on,
The hero's lads have stayed behind,
Come let us join him, in his bounty!'
The fair Anat retorts:
'Consider well, Captain Yatpan!
20   Consider well, retract your answer!
I will transform you, I will mould you,
An eagle for my quiver,
A shaft live at my waist.
When Aqhat sits to eat,
Daniel's son to dine,
Eagles will be circling,
Flocks gathering, poised, soaring.
I will drift among the eagles,
Steady you over Aqhat,
30   Then strike! Twice on the skull, thrice round the ears!
As the veins burst, as the blood surges,
As he is butchered on his knees –
His soul will vanish like the wind,
His spirit like a breath,
Like cloud in his nostrils.
He will not live!'
The Mistress moulds Captain Yatpan,
an eagle for her quiver,
A shaft live at her waist.
40   Aqhat sat down to eat,
Daniel's son to dine.
Above him eagles circling,
Flocks gathered, poised, soaring.

28

Among the eagles drifts Anat,
Over Aqhat she steadies him,
He strikes! Twice on the skull, thrice round the ears!
As the veins burst, as the blood surges,
His knees give way: thus is he butchered.
His soul vanishes like the wind,
50 His spirit like a breath,
Like cloud in his nostrils.
Anat, as his strength failed,
Weeps for Aqhat:
'Life would I give you,
         . . . for your bow . . .
  for your quiver
Could you but breathe.'
The flocks wheeled, vanished,
The eagles.

III

(the first five lines are broken)

She bows down
         . . . in the midst of waters
She prostrates herself
. . . broken is the bow,
      eight arrows in a quiver.
Anat the fair, the flawless Virgin,
Sister-in-law of sorrowing peoples,
Took up the burden, thus she grieved:
'O furrow, furrow, chant 'How bitter!'
10 His delicate hands, those of a singer,
The grace of his fingers, touching the harp;
In his mouth pearls are decaying,
Derelict teeth, held fast in death;
Nothing grows and the young grass withers,
Dry as the heart of ancient trees.

His two companions raise the cry,
The Lay of Aqhat plaintive sing,
The burden 'How bitter! How bitter!'
I killed him for his folly like a dog,
20   A baleful viper, nesting in the wall;
I killed him, coveting his bow,
I would not spare him for his quiver.
But his bow is lost to me –
And now his murder blights the summer,
Fruits shrivel, and the sap grows sour,
The kernel in the unripe corn.'
   Now Daniel, man of healing,
Lord of the Shades, of Harnam,
Rose, sat at the flared gate,
30   The threshing floor, superb with princes.
He judged the widow justly,
The orphan's grievance fairly,
When, lifting up his eyes,
He saw Pughat, his daughter,
Who fills the pitchers, gathers dew,
Knows the courses of the stars.
She looked round, gazed:
Barley in the threshing-floor,
Dry, blasted; drooping vines,
40   Faded blossoms in the vineyards.
Over her father's dwelling,
Eagles were circling, flocks gathering.
She weeps; her heart is sore;
Shaken by sobs, she tears
The robe of Daniel, man of healing,
Cloak of the valiant lord of Harnam.
And Daniel, man of healing,
Invoked dark clouds, deep magic,
Spells to assuage the heat:
50   'Come clouds, rain on the summer fruit,
Come dew, light on the tender grapes.
For seven years will Baal be wanting,

Eight, the Rider of Storm-Clouds?
Will the dew fail, the downpours cease,
The deep springs be silent,
Baal's music, the thunder, be hushed?'
He tears his robe, the man of healing,
His cloak, the valiant lord of Harnam,
And to his daughter loudly cries:
60 'Hear me, Pughat, who fetches water,
Gathers dew to swell the barley,
Knows the courses of the stars.
Saddle my ass,
Prepare its harness,
Its traces of silver,
Its trappings of gold.'
Pughat obeys, fetcher of water,
Who gathers dew to swell the barley,
Who knows the courses of the stars.
70 She harnesses the ass, weeping,
Reins it and saddles it, weeping,
She helps her father mount, weeping,
On the ass's back she lifts him,
Strong and supple, the beast's back.
Smartly he goes, off to the meadow.
Daniel sees a green stem rising
In the bare meadow,
In soil exhausted, cracked and parched,
A green stem rising.
80 He kisses, caresses the green stem:
'Flourish, green stem, in the bare meadow,
Where all else withers, flourish, green stem!
May gracious Aqhat gather you,
Store sweet grass in the granary!'
He turned then to the ashen fields.
An ear had sprouted in the field,
Was ripening in the seared soil.
The ear he kisses, caresses:
'May the ear flourish in the field,

31

90   May the corn ripen in the earth,
        May gracious Aqhat gather you,
        Store you, sweet grain, in the granary!'
          Even as he was speaking,
        While words still crossed his lips,
        He lifted up his eyes, discerned
        Men approaching, Aqhat missing.
        The two companions came alone
        Aqhat was absent! They came back!
        Twice and thrice they clapped their crowns,
100   Their ears resounded from their blows,
        Their hair was loose, their locks awry,
        Their curls were cropped, close to the temples.
        They shed their tears like quarter-shekels,
        And as they came, they cried:
        'In Baal's hands are our fortunes cast,
        The hands of Sapan deal weal and woe;
        We bear, alas, grave tidings.
        What shall we say, sad heralds to Daniel?
        The blows against his battered head,
110   The broken temples of our master,
        How Anat made his spirit flee,
        His soul, Yatpan, like wind, like vapour?'
        They came, their voices rose,
        They cried out, shrilly:
        'Hear, Daniel, man of healing!
        Aqhat is dead, the valiant hero:
        The fair Anat drew out his soul
        Like wind, his life like vapour.'
        His feet unsteady, his face flushed,
120   His back a-quiver, doubled-over,
        Knotted with pain in his entrails,
        Daniel cried out, his voice rose bitter:
        'May he who slew my son die also! . . .'

(six lines missing)

He gazed far off, he watched them coming,

Eagles in flight out of the west.
He lifted up his voice and cried:
'The wings of eagles may Baal sunder,
Sunder, O Baal, their wings in flight!
May they fall to my feet,
That I might comb their crop,
That I might see if there is fat,
If there is bone; then I would weep,
And I would bury him,
In crannies of the earth-gods leave him.'
    As he was speaking,
While words still crossed his lips,
Baal shattered the wings of eagles,
Baal broke their wings in flight.
They dropped, fell to his feet,
He combed their crops, he found –
No fat, no bone!
He lifted up his voice and cried:
'The wings of eagles may Baal quicken,
Quicken, O Baal, their wings in flight!'
Healed, eagles flew, wings whirred.
As he watched, eyes aloft, scanning,
Hurgab he saw, Father of eagles.
He lifted up his voice and cried:
'The wings of Hurgab may Baal sunder,
Sunder, O Baal, his wings in flight!
May he fall to my feet,
That I might comb his crop,
That I might see if there is fat,
If there is bone; then I would weep,
And I would bury him,
In crannies of the earth-gods leave him.'
    As he was speaking,
While words still crossed his lips,
Baal shattered the wings of Hurgab,
Baal broke his wings in flight.
He dropped, fell to his feet.

130

140

150

160

He combed his crop – he found
No fat, no bone!
He lifted up his voice and cried:
'The wings of Hurgab may Baal quicken,
Quicken, O Baal, his wings in flight!'
Healed, Hurgab flew, wings whirred.
　　As he watched, eyes aloft, scanning,
Semel he saw, Mother of eagles.
170　He lifted up his voice and cried:
'The wings of Semel may Baal sunder,
Sunder, O Baal, her wings in flight!
May she fall to my feet,
That I might comb her crop,
That I might see if there is fat,
If there is bone; then I would weep,
And I would bury him,
In crannies of the earth-gods leave him.'
　　As he was speaking,
180　While words still crossed his lips,
Baal shattered the wings of Semel,
Baal broke her wings in flight.
She dropped, fell to his feet,
He combed her crop,
He found there was fat, there was bone –
From there he drew Aqhat,
He held him,
He wept and buried,
Buried him deep in darkness.
190　He wept, with piercing voice
He cried:
'The wings of eagles may Baal shatter,
Shatter, O Baal, their wings in flight,
If they fly over my son's grave,
And snatch him from his sleep!'
　　Over Qor-Mayim the king cried:
'Woe to you, Well of Waters!
For noble Aqhat, slain by you,

34

Be like an exile in El's house,
200 A fugitive now and for ever,
Now and for evermore!'
   He took his staff and travelled further,
He reached Mararat-Me'ullal-Bener,
With piercing voice he cried:
'Woe to you, Bitter-under-Yoke,
For noble Aqhat, slain by you,
On earth may no root thrust from you,
Bow your head under ruthless hands,
A fugitive now and for ever,
210 Now and for evermore!'
   He took his staff and travelled further,
He reached Qeret-Abilim,
Weeping City of the Moon;
With piercing voice he cried:
'Woe to you, Weeping City!
For noble Aqhat, slain by you,
May Baal scourge you with blindness,
For this age and for ever,
Now and for evermore!'
220 He took his staff, and travelled further,
Daniel approached his house,
His palace Daniel entered.
His rooms filled with weepers,
His halls with women wailing,
Self-lacerators groaned.
They wept for noble Aqhat,
For Daniel's lost child sobbed,
For the man of healing,
Days, months, months, years,
230 For seven years they wept.
For noble Aqhat tears,
For Daniel's darling shed,
The man of healing, seven years.
   Then Daniel, man of healing, spoke;
The valiant Harnamite resolved;

He lifted up his voice and cried:
'Go, weepers, from my palace,
Women wailing, from my courts,
Lacerators, go!'
240   He sacrificed, invoked the gods,
His offering rose to the heavens,
The Harnamite's gift to the stars.
    He welcomed to his house
Singers, with drum and cymbal,
Musicians, dancers glistening.
Pughat then spoke, fetcher of water:
'My father has invoked the gods,
The incense rises to the heavens,
The incense to the lords of stars!
250   O bless me, that my way be blessed!
Succour me, that my way be sure!
That I may kill my brother's killer,
Requite the murder of our child!'
    Then Daniel, man of healing, spoke:
'May Pughat live, fetcher of water,
Who gathers dew to swell the barley,
Who knows the courses of the stars.
Well may she prosper!
May she kill her brother's killer,
260   Requite the murder of our child!'
    She took a creature from the sea,
She washed herself and dyed herself,
Reddened herself with the sea-whelk's harvest,
That stains the myriad tracts of ocean.
She dressed herself in man's attire,
And wore a shirt above her armour;
She had a sword sheathed in a scabbard,
And covered it in women's clothes.
The Lamp of Gods had run its course,
270   When Pughat came to busy fields,
The Lamp of Gods, Shapash, was setting,
When Pughat reached the clustered tents.

The word was brought to Captain Yatpan:
'Our patron is in your headquarters,
       . . . has entered the precincts.'
Yatpan exclaimed, the hired Captain:
'Take her, and she shall serve me wine,
Wine for my cup,
Drink for my flagon!'
280   They took Pughat, who served him wine,
Wine for his cup,
Drink for his flagon.
      Then Yatpan bragged, the Mistress' vassal:
'Wine, O my Lady, makes me fearless,
I am invincible, my Lady!
A god, like El, Master of nomads!
The hand that struck down noble Aqhat
Will slay your thousand foes, my Lady!'
      She wove a spell over the tents,
290   Her heart's desire she knew was granted.
A second time she filled his cup,
Stirring the mixture as before,
But now she spiced his cup with poison,
Quenching his thirst . . .

(The tablet breaks off at this point)

IV

THE REPHAIM TEXTS

(Of the sequel, only the following fragments have survived. They are very obscure, and except for the last, entirely broken. There is no clear sequence; I have put the best last. Fragments ii and iii, iv and v belong to the same tablets.

(i)   'O Spirits, Spirits,
        Come to my house, enter my dwelling,
        I cry to you, I summon you,

37

Immortal powers to my palace.
Light-footed Shades, come thither!
Come quickly ghosts, come thither!
O healing Shades, Spirits my friends,
Now I begin a thirty days' journey,
To reach my house, enter my palace.'
10   And El declared: 'O Spirits, Spirits,
Come to my house, enter my dwelling.
I cry to you, I summon you,
Immortal powers to my palace.
Light-footed Shades, come thither!
Come quickly ghosts, come thither!

(ii)   '. . . in my house,
. . . seven, eight in my palace.
Light-footed Shades, come thither!
Come quickly ghosts, come thither!'
Horses are reined,
Harnessed to chariots,
They mount the chariots,
Swift are the stallions.
One day they ride, two days,
10   On the third day, at sunrise,
The Spirits reach the threshing-floors,
The ghosts come to the planted fields.
Then Daniel, man of healing, spoke,
Lord of the Shades, of Harnam, cried:
'The spirits in the threshing-floors,
Immortal wraiths in planted fields,
The ghostly powers come to eat,
Feast them . . .
              . . . apples and nectar,
20   Attentive . . .'

(iii)   . . . The Shades sacrifice . . .
              . . . the immortals feast
                . . . like men who die

38

into the mystery
you come
. . . on a summer's day
. . . the spirits feed
ghosts drink
. . . god of the elixir
10   . . . Offer up a lamb

(iv)   'They come, they come, the godlike spirits,
Visit my palace, reach my house.'
And Daniel said: 'O Spirits, Spirits,
Come to my house, enter my dwelling!
I cry to you, I summon you,
Immortal powers to my palace.
Light-footed Shades, come thither!
Come quickly ghosts, come thither!
Thumuq is there, the Wraith of Baal,
10   The troops of Baal, Anat's warriors.
O Spirits, wraiths, come to my house,
I cry to you, I summon you,
Immortal powers to my palace.
The hosts of hell are rustling there,
His Majesty, the Shadow-King.
Listen, Shades, listen! Spirits, hear!
Anoint his head with fragrant oil,
Vow fealty . . .
Let Aqhat reign! My son be king!
20   Ascend my throne, Lord of Amor,
The sovereign seat hold in his sway.
I call the Shades, invoke the Spirits,
Into my house, heart of my palace.
Light-footed Shades, come thither!
Come quickly ghosts, come thither!
Horses are reined,
Harnessed to chariots,
They mount the chariots,
Swift are the stallions.

30   One day they ride, two days,
      On the third day, at sunrise,
      The spirits reach the threshing-floors,
      The ghosts come to the planted fields . . .

(v)   There is your son!
       Son after son crowds to the place!
       Look at your hands!
       See how your lips kiss the lost child!
       Shoulder to shoulder brothers bustle,
       Start up together, roused by El.
       In El's name, flesh forms, and the dead appear,
       The valiant young men his Name's blessing quickens.
       Thumuq is there, the Wraith of Baal,
10   The troops of Baal, Anat's warriors;
       The hosts of hell are rustling there,
       His Majesty, the Shadow-King;
       As when Anat is chasing fowl,
       And all the flocks fly up to heaven.
       Oxen and sheep he killed for them,
       He slaughtered bulls and excellent rams,
       Yearlings he butchered, suckling lambs,
       With kids in droves. And as they enter,
       They see the silvery olive oil,
20   The golden . . . welcomes them,
       Fruit on the table in the hall,
       The royal hall.
       That day he served them wine from *Tmk*,
       Superb fresh wine, frothing for princes,
       Light clear wine, joyous wine!
       Wine like a necklace of red gems
       Encircling Lebanon,
       The dew of vintage sprung from El.
       The Spirits feasted all that day,
30   The next day too, eating and drinking.
       A third day, a fourth day passed likewise,
       A fifth, a sixth, eating and drinking,

The Shades were feasted in the hall.
Each day into the Lebanon
Wine poured, libations on its slopes.
    Then on the seventh day . . .
            . . . Victorious Baal . . .
            . . . his friend, my father . . .

Notes

I.

A legend of the righteous Daniel was current in late Biblical times, as shown by the references to him in Ezekiel 14 and 28.3. There is of course no discernable relationship with the Book of Daniel. Daniel's epithet, *mt rpi*, means both 'man of healing' and 'Lord of the Shades', for the cure of sickness implies an intimacy with death; healing powers are often chthonic powers. A good example of this is Asculepius (cf. M. Astour *Hellenosemitica* p.205-10, 313-16). If, in the Rephaim texts, Daniel summons the Shades in order to resurrect Aqhat, the relationship becomes entirely clear. Later, in the Bible, the Shades, or Rephaim, came to be identified with an extinct race of indigenous giants, of whom Og of Bashan was the last survivor.

A town of Harnam is known from Egyptian sources. Others speculate that it is Haran, whence Abraham came.

I. i. 1-21.

The practice of sleeping in sacred precincts in order to be visited by the god is known all over the Middle East, and has many variants. It is technically termed an incubation ritual.

I. i. 23.

El in the Ugaritic epics is the remote high god, usually approached through intermediaries, of whom Baal (lit. 'Lord') is the most important, especially in this context, since he is the protector of humanity, and god of rain and fertility. El had no temple in Ugarit, whereas Baal's was of great splendour.

I. i. 32.

Elsewhere Baal's father is named as Dagan, whom we know from the Bible as the god of the Philistines. Strangely, Dagan plays no part in the epics, even though he had a prominent temple. 'God' is the literal translation of El, which I have used occasionally. The bull, as the symbol of potency, represents the male godhead all over the Eastern Mediterranean.

I. i. 37.

Solar disks, sometimes winged, were engraved on tombstones in Syria and Anatolia (following the interpretation of M. Isevat, "Traces of Hittite at the beginning of the Ugaritic Epic of Aqhat," *Ugarit Forschungen* 3 (1971) 351.

I. ii. 35.

An illusion to these conception and childbirth deities is to be found in one of the most mysterious of the Psalms, Psalm 68. (v.7). God liberates the bound 'with Kosharot ("Ug. K<u>t</u>r → Heb. Kšr"). I do not know why they are associated with swallows, though the interpretation is accepted by most, though not all, authorities. The Kathirat play an important part in celebrating the marriage of Nikkal and the Moon, in another Ugaritic poem.

I. iii. 15,17.
Kothar-wa-Hasis is a composite deity (wa = and), like many in Ugarit. For instance, we have a messenger god known as Vine-and-Field, and a ritual scapegoat called Death-and-Evil. This is one reason for rejecting the hoary critical assumption that the two names of God stand for two different traditions, Yahwist and Elohist.

I. iii. 29.
In Ugaritic, the domain of Kothar-wa-Hasis is called Hkpt. The identification with Memphis, in Egypt, the city sacred to Ptah, has been questioned, largely because elsewhere their home is stated to be Kaphtor, probably Crete. On the other hand, the two lands correspond to the double name of the god, who dwells in the two principal centres of fine craftsmanship of the time – Egypt and Minoan Crete. Incidentally, from *Hkpt* is derived our word for Egypt, through the Greek *Aigyptos*.

I. iv. 3.
The salting and spicing of carving knives is still widely practised in the Near East.

I. iv. 41-2.
Anat's epithet is still completely obscure.

I. iv. 51.
We possess the text and stage-directions of a ritual drama in Ugarit, 'The Birth of the Good and Gracious Gods'. (UT 68).

I. iv. 58-65.
The whole of this passage turns on a pun between the words for 'death' and 'man'.

II. i. 1.
Some scholars resist the interpretation of btlt (cf. Hebrew *betula*) as 'Virgin', simply because she wasn't. She indulges in some rather extravagant intercourse with her half-brother Baal, assuming the form of a cow for the purpose. But such paradoxical goddesses abound in the Ancient Near East – Inanna, Ishtar,

Artemis etc. (cf. Marvin Pope *The Song of Songs:* The Anchor Bible 7c, (Doubleday, New York, 1976) p.167 ff.) The most conspicuous examples are Kali in India and the Virgin Mary herself.

II. i. 27-8.
De Moor considers this to be a formal proposal of marriage. (UF7, p.194). In Harran, at this period, husband and wife were formally called brother and sister.

II. ii. 6-10.
Quite incoherent.

II. ii. 11.
Yatpan's epithet has also been interpreted as 'the drunken warrior' and 'the Sutu warrior'. The Sutu were nomads on the fringe of the desert, who were often hired as mercenaries, when they were not pillaging.

II. ii. 15
De Moor believes that this is the wedding feast.

II. ii. 24.
Aistleitner holds that she tucked Yatpan in her vagina – a most uncomfortable suggestion.

III. 10-20.
As an illustration of the astonishing divergence of interpretation, one may take this version, by B. Margalit, 'Studia Ugaritica II', Ugarit Forschungen 8 (1976) p.169-172. Margalit reads the whole passage as an account of a descent to the underworld, not as a lament at all.

> her hands are like a torch
> her fingers like a lamp
> she extracts the stones of his mouth,
> she seizes his teeth and consumes them.
> On the crown of his head she puts a groove
> in accordance with the will of the chthonic deities
> and the instruction of the pit-dwellers.
> And from his pit Aqhat beholds,
> he sees the black of darkness.
> Yea, a giant viper is at the gates,
> A dog at its sceptre-side.

III. 24-5.
The season may be March or April, when the last rains are important for the crops.

III. 34.
Pughat simply means 'girl'. The *gh* is a harsh guttural, which English readers need not bother to pronounce. Incidentally, the *H* in Kothar-wa-Hasis is somewhat like the *ch* in 'loch'.

III. 53.
Baal's most common epithet, as the storm god. It is borrowed by God in the same Psalm, Psalm 68.

III. 106.
Sapan is 'the northern (mountain)', Mt. Casius, the Ugaritic Olympus. Here Baal had his home, which became synonymous with him. Occasionally, in the Bible, the same idiom is used of God; for instance, in Psalm 48.3, Zion is, inappropriately enough, 'the remote parts of the north'.

III. 196,203,212.
All these names are directly translated. The only one whose meaning is very doubtful is Mararat-Me'ullal-Bener. The interpretation is de Moor's. (Ugarit Forschungen 7 p.209-10): 'The bitter one brought under the yolk'.

III. 225.
Self-laceration was a Canaanite custom, as we see from its prohibition in the Bible. In the famous contest between Elijah and the priests of Baal, the latter lacerated themselves to arouse Baal's sympathy.

III. 261-4.
The same verses describe Anat's 'toilette', (UAB 8 p.92-3), before indulging in one of her gruesome massacres. This has given rise to the hypothesis that Pughat here disguises herself as Anat. Red dye was for men, yellow dye for women.

III. 269,271.
Shapash, the sun-goddess.

The last section, concerning Pughat's enterprise, is extremely ambiguous. In my version (following *Textes Ougaritiques* p.408 and de Moor Ugarit Forschungen 7 p.212), Pughat disguises herself as Anat, and knows that Yatpan is the murderer. Yatpan, drunk, and believing her to be Anat, flouts the laws of hospitality, and brags that he is El's equal and invincible. His hubris seals his fate.

Other commentators consider Pughat not to be in disguise, and unaware of Yatpan's guilt. She come to enlist him in her search for the murderer. He serves her wine, but is drunk enough to boast of killing Aqhat. I find this a bit unconvincing.

45

Michael Astour, finally, believes that the scene is a reconciliation. (Hellenosemitica 74-75).

IV. iv. 15.
'The Nameless One', Death, King of the Underworld. The reading, however, is very tentative.

IV. iv. 19.
Only the beginning of each line in this column is preserved; and 'let Aqhat reign' is in a lacuna. Hence the identification of the king is pure, if intelligent, speculation.